The Needle
Regan Good
978-1-934639-30-6

First Edition, First Printing 2020
Printed in the USA

Published by Harry Tankoos Books

Distributed to the trade by
Small Press Distribution
1341 Seventh Street
Berkeley, CA 94710
www.spdbooks.org

Cataloging-in-publication data
is available from the Library of Congress.

Cover and book design by Brandon Saloy

THE NEEDLE

REGAN GOOD

HARRY TANKOOS BOOKS

2020

TABLE OF CONTENTS

Gratitude to Michael Scharf for publishing *The Needle*, and previously *The Atlantic House*. All my love to Andrew Hultkrans, the best man I know. And love and blessings to Brandon Saloy, Claudia Keelan, Miranda Field, Tom Thompson, Saskia Hamilton, Timea Szell, Holly Amos, and Jason Zuzga.

For Sean Richard Good, my brother

TO THE PIANO BURNING ON THE BEACH

Now I have enjoyed a perfect exhilaration
(that was part and parcel of God)
as I call Nature and the words of Jesus
Christ as they are, printed in red.
Such was the cacophony and calamity
of the burning instrument, sounding like a harp
strummed by strikes of wind and fire.
(No plinking toy, as the piano's wire strings
mimicked the sound of the Celestial Spheres
grinding against the Great Chain.)
Sea winds, not fingers, fanned the flames.
(Though to us it sounded as if someone *played*.)
The hottest flames produced the highest notes,
and blasts of sand made percussion of the keys.
Loose sands plucked grace notes on the strings.
The piano—burning in stages and in parts—made
more complex music than Earth had ever heard.
Its upright lid crashed down in an explosion
of crazy fireballs the piney woods sucked in.
Sprung wires snapped and echoed in the updrafts;
they made a whining sound jerking in the air,
like the mourning of a hundred violins.
In the middle of such chaos, the Gnostic Jesus said,
"If you bring forth what is within you, it will save you.
If you have nothing within you, you will die."

The burning piano made such music the entire time,
burning in its sandy centrifuge, it made a Dresden
of its fire hole as the diurnal tide came in.
Water changed the tonal quality of the sound,
and softened what was a sustained fortissimo.
Some said the waves themselves then played the keys,
but by midnight the instrument was mostly gone.
Tides still breathed through the strings, like an underwater harp
resembling accordioned filter-plates of baleen.

WE WENT HUNTING OF AN EVENING

To find the morning wanting. Lit a fire in the sun.
Then burned for Easter last year's Christmas evergreen.

In that unwholesome air, our faces flushed.
(*Heat will leach the sickness out,* we thought,
as when a needle nicks a sour hoof
to drain putrescence from a bulb of rot.)

Ducks grew horns here, and their beaks were sealed with slime.

Their necks were weak and creased. They flopped.
We often pulled them up to watch them drop.

Is this the meat we eat? we asked ourselves.

We plucked them bald, pinning back their skins with poultry pins.
Their cavities we filled with woodland mice and monarch wings.
We milked a muddy broth from fatless bones,
then candied broken livers with lemon rinds.
Ramps and scapes we braided to embolden the fumet.
We soaked the cowl of deckle meat in a sun-warmed bain-marie.
Its despumated froth we turned into a jellied consommé.
Three robins' eggs were scrambled for a fiddlehead soufflé.
We crisped each duck tongue in snail fat, rendered in a common pail.
Their brains we whisked in bright green cooking oil,
then we brothed with wine the clottings of the fond.

We wasted nothing so that we would not want.
We ate until the air was full of fur, in fact.
And in such triumph, the sickness rose and fled.

We made a somber march to the spot where our good
dog died and the gaseous skunk grass grew.
Down the sloping grass to the flooded place
where the accidental daffodils fed—
the pale wild ones, papery and nearly white.
Primordial ghosts (so pure and spare), they suck
brown waters through translucent pipes.

We'd drowned catlings here each spring.
And place the wreath into the pool, to watch it hiss and spin.
We longed to be good but were only guilty, at our best.
Not for our riches, but for our faults.
Our goodness gone because we lived.

THE SAILOR CANNOT SEE THE NORTH, BUT HE KNOWS THE NEEDLE CAN

It was a monument in the dark: a polished needle
on the side yard of the nineteenth-century estate
by the plaster swimming pool, behind the pines.
It was like a weathervane, a compass, or a clock.

The wind could move it, and so could we.

Near midnight, we pointed its sharp end pondward
(where the dead children were said to swing)
and pushed one heavy-butted end deeply down …

The stars, the highway, the empty white pool
made a large and windy room for the whirling blade
to spin, as it was, mounted on a pin,
hinged to swing in all directions.

The needle made a whirling hum.
It was a silky planchette in its glide.
(It took no real heft to make it go.)
Balanced by a counter-levered weight
—a bulbous ballast wrapped in black electrical tape—
the needle moved nearly effortlessly
and simultaneously careened crazily.

We marveled how so light a touch ignited everything.

Near midnight on New Year's Eve, we took the needle
and threw it down.

It pointed not just toward north or south or east or west.
But to all the points without exacting names, the interstitial
directions in-between.

The needle swung and spun, and we laughed
at its spasmodically delirious directionlessness.
We thrilled to be so free and yet so focused on a single point.
Midnight: it was a whirling needle in the dark,
making sounds of hoisting sails, whine of industry,
a dry, neglected, unoiled joint—a work of art.
The needle was the central engine for everything!
It climbs, crests, falls, dips, then climbs back up again.
Better to simultaneously hold two opposing ideas,
like happiness and sorrow, in one's mind together,
than to believe a single needle points to anything.

BACK IN THE PROVINCE LANDS

Back in the Province Lands, its low-sunken mounds
plateau to higher grounds, presenting to a body
a swarming vista of berry, branch, scrub, and pine.
Monochromatic blacks from the beforeyears,
redolent and present, some gone yellow in the afteryears,
as evermore churns grains and winds upward and away.
Sands piled to peaks, those peaks scored to hollows, holes,
varied mounds of heretofore and nevermore. Eternal
accumulation scatters and humps, white upon white.
In the in-between times, black wrack shrinks to a leathery hide.
One can still pop the rubber pods for their amber slime.
Forked, vascular *Sertularia,* fern garlands, and rockweed:
all bleed viscous syrups that feed the sugar kelp.
Dead-man's-fingers, glasswort, spike grass, that spiny sour weed!
Seaweeds zigzag on the beach at the outer reaches of the waves.
Steam rises from these sunbaked welter-cakes.
Avoid the stinking whale intestines popping on the sand.
Look for lumps of ambergris, regurgitated gold.
Haul off full skirts of baleen, those massive sieves
accordioned like crinoline or a string of barrel staves.
Like monsters on a seventeenth-century sovereign map,
tendriled terrors surge up, though it is the whales
who are the giant cattle of the sea.
Their ape-like eyes sunk in wrinkled, baggy human lids.
They turn and loll, and sometimes they breach wholly in the air.
Waterspouts like fireworks or faraway Ferris wheels.

The buoyant whales are mourning as they sing.
They feed their calves lumpish stinking curds for milk
as they glide over a thousand grounded crafts,
figureheaded boats and blunt-nosed vessels—all lagan,
                                        hulls and masts,
mossy, sodden, and infested black with sucking, waving plants.

Moisture rolls off the banks, making a foggy scrim:
walk directly into it, carrying a V-shaped divining rod
to detect pure water from a spring—here, saltwater changes
everything: the dead bird, half bone, half feathers still.
The shaft of one strong feather—split and curled.

WE WASHED OUR NAPKINS AT THE SODA LAKE

Because the door still smelled of death, we
could not cross, for the stench and slipperiness.
Because odor enters into a fabric's weave,
we lifted up our skirts of earthy crinoline,
then scrubbed the saddle down with mint.

Flecked with gory crud, our bad cat deposited a gift.

We preferred outdoor waters to those piped in.
(Inside waters scaled the pipes and hardened hair.
Our soaps were neutered and would not froth.)
Outside, the waters were blank and soft,
          milky white, rolling with gentle salt.
(In summer, the rocks cupped us as the waterfall
drove floats to the bottom of the pit—sticks,
most beautifully boiled, bobbed up
                    clean and slippery like a child
                              flayed of every strip of skin.
We often gathered them for kindling
                    then "burned the baby-bones in Spring.")

Our darling kitten's nutsack had been clipped,
while the other's stomach has gone to flab—
it swings—a rubber curtain when she trots.

We swept brown and black feathers into a pile,
then transferred bits of wing and leg onto a trowel.
(The central headless core I flipped into a flowerpot.)
With frost, our gift kept fresh and nearly odorless.

Tonight these cats grind their glandular faces into ours,
purring throaty percolations of fake love. Hungry
for offalic fish, they drink can-rendered meats
from the vivid pockets of their pores—then drop
to sleep, hunting mice with twitching paws.
Unlike the thing outside, immobile and vanishing,
becoming hard in parts, and elsewhere liquefied.
At the lake, soap was not a panacea against the soil,
just as mint could not completely clean our door.
Each time the cats mewl for out, they linger at this rim—
then they vault the minted saddle to murder more.

COAL PILES BY THE GOWANUS CANAL: THE CORBELS OF COIGNET

Your lightweight concrete was a sugar shell,
one poured instead of carved, I thought, as our skiff spun
in circles, one-oared, in the viscous eau de Nile—

From the Italianate window of the Renaissance Easter
Egg, one spied with telescopes this little city grow
from stream to humping hill—a kingdom of varied
industry by the bulwarks and the graving docks.
Bowed promontories were built with scraggle grass
woven into weirs the color of ochre marmalade.

Once a Sachem fed deeply from a living water well.

Now violet creosote chars and oily motes feed a greasy snake
whose head is buried further west in a giant sulphurous egg.

O Coignet! Some soul threw a dozen oysters in the drink,
mimicking the lightness of the paste and the scope
of your weightless dream!

Here, this river threads itself through the Medieval arch,
by the palisades, the faded planks, then under the BQE,
where metal scraps have been divided into light and dark.

What purpose the little arch? To divide the water into a two-tined fork?

Water doesn't thread like a needle, Coignet, one cannot knot it to a stopping ball.

It's a living gas, our stunted Thames, our River Styx.
The Boatmen know how water makes its constant way.
The water moves through the arch and rejoins itself.
A mended mind. A confluence of rolling time.

Our skiff floats above the mercuries and iron darks.
The liver-colored contaminates of the purple pond,
                    a liver-colored sluice of liver loams.
Does the water rejoin itself in glory? Bring us asunder.
The little boat cannot pass through, oily snake, for you are hungry.
The pylons hug the water and the waste,
                                        the waste of the material world?
Through its industrial fingers, the water is being eaten by the world,
                                        the world is being eaten by the world.
Or at least that is as it seems—since you last rode here,
Monsieur Coignet, they have filled in all the streams.

TO THE SAUGATUCK RIVER AND ITS SOURCE AT SUGAR HOLLOW, WESTPORT, CONNECTICUT

Morning river-sounds and building-sounds. Knocks
and bangs of wooden beams spinning on chains in air.
By the highway, the half-buried water well is a little house
next to the upturned root system of a druid's dream.
This is the river that flows out from its source.
Then under Peter's Bridge, under the train trestle,
past the blue and white sailboats of Stony Point.
This river bends by the pedestrian path, flows past
the benches dedicated to our library's doyens.
The riverhead, its mouth of shaggy gaseous banks,
disgorges onto the mosquitoey island of Cockenoe,
then moves out farther than one can see from shoreline or from dock.
River like a crepuscular cowl, a gray-furred animal
with alien eyes hunting warm-blooded morning mice.
Overnight it snowed a 1970s snow and the river froze,
turning Riverside into a tunnel of towering beatitudes.
The juncture of Imperial and Post is now a frozen world.
Past the Masonic Temple, right-angled to our oldest
clapboard church, all the town's life a toile on a winter hill,
sledding as if there were no such thing as Death and Rot.
The emerald-headed mallard and his nest-colored mate
bundle mulch and feathers on an icy shelf and wait.
Abundant blood in the leaves and in their histories.
The stone walls running through dense woods
are like Roman ships built inside the Coliseum.

Or a paper ship pulled upright inside a bottle.
Now half done, behind my head, the river moves.
Saugatuck, river of the Paugussett—tribe of the tidal flats.
I sleep at angles to its feeding streams that flow
imperceptibly underneath my borrowed bed.
I lie against the direction they move: downhill,
as the dying deer lies still, head under its heart.
When it dies, where does it go? Into the Saugatuck,
the wide-open mouth of movement and flow.
Eventually it will be flushed out past Cockenoe.
But its hooves and bones return full circle to the Sound.
If this had been your town, you would understand.

BY ORDER OF THE EASTERN STAR

By the Rings of Hester and the Armies of Ruth!
By emblems of biblical heroines and lopsided brick
molds, needles, and roped weights. Roster marks
defined your comportment by systems and degrees.
And so by continual refinements you advanced.
In this assembly, your sisters were ever angels, Mother.
Each in white floaty dresses turned black by time.
The fathers carried calipers and flathead trowels.
They laid the paving stones and built the domiciles.
In secrecy and togetherness, you were never Widow
Mother, only Star Point initiate and Rainbow Girl.
Fairest among Ten Thousand, Altogether Lovely,
an orchid corsage straight-pinned to your fatal bib.
The color ladder you climbed led to a pot of pagan gold.
With your white-buck Pocahontas apron and a book of rules,
you extended beyond your station, until all of Egypt
lapped at your slippered feet. The lion drew its beaded
jaw along the mud, startled by your smell, and fled.
Your future was Damask Rose and Lily of the Valley.
A Yankee Doodle fair with blue and red sugar cones.
All Blue Willow swallows turning over a wooden bridge.
One was promised gold armatures in every water well,
and leafy celery stalks in an etched and fluted glass.
A failing brass-hearted Patron undermined your Electra.
With you well dressed in the house of Dutch Reform, facing east,
the belfry called the poor through its doors and married them.

Witnessed by the Dutch buried in their autumn graves.
By the orders invested in the elected and in the webby dross:
will you or won't you wind your worm's way through the core?
O Sister of Hope, what is the Season called where you are?

WE MEET UPON THE LEVEL AND WE PART UPON THE SQUARE: MASONS IN THE FAMILY RECALLED BY A GOWANUS BRICK YARD

No one in this barn-like world painted Depression-era green.
The backyard was a dooryard where obscene roses grew.
Common leaves turned gold in the poisoned creek.
From acrid tomatoes and their stringent, itchy leaves,
much raw magic met the curbside and the underlings.
They met here on the foursquare, by the wormy overhang.
Like a piedmont was the spiritual climb, and once arrived,
all was greener than Egypt and her slippery son, the Nile.
By all municipal ordinances and recorders of the streets!
Here the ground was measured with a weight and string.
Here they built a bank and here they paved a street.
Here, a fence of iron tridents molded in the shape of grapes.

Now, red paint erupts in curls down to pale, pink brick.

This is the fertile crescent of their fruitless progeny.

Square, Level, Tassel, and Tie. The Great Architect squares
our actions to our deeds, then He levels off our lives.

Goodbye from the corner and from the dried-out cabochons.
Goodbye to the opiates in the drains, the hemlock of these waterways.
Goodbye to the citron burns, and to the vines that left a stain.
(One vine is actually painted to ensure it's forever green.)

Corsage pins rusted the white gowns of all the Fatal Girls,
girls braceleted to death with tiny pearls, their bangles
curled around their wrists like vinegar worms.
Pearls sunk in tight bands like doll teeth in a platinum trough.
You cannot pick them out to search their undersides for rot.

Real vines climbed, branched, to leave a figure from scorched juice.
Ivy climbs the sandy bricks and shoots itself into the loam.
Elsewhere a cat-paw hammer pulls a nail cleanly from its hole.

THE FABRIC: BOMBAZINE, WORSTED AND WARPED

These coffin corners jammed with jonquils!
Like hyenas, those birds-of-paradise,
or strange billed waterfowl, ravaged
by the taintworm, the flesh-hungry worm,
eating open a pelican's raw red eye.
Cherry-lipped mucal balls of berry
engender the worst, the woof, and the wolf.
I know why the yew and the willow.
Jet jewels are to retard the rain
since they steal the shine of the living.
Let us retard the winter crust and exalt the summer web!
An *ash* sheds its leaves in the winter,
while the *yew* remains green forever.
We bring flowers to the mourning lamb
who tucks its hooves under its heart and stands
for all the dead babies in Babyland.
Marble pound cakes frosted with extruded
curlicues of sugar paste in pastel hues.
The dull beads of thy cremation locket
(carved both from the oak tree and its seed),
reject the shine of the blistered baby lip.
Those beads are dirt and dust, not jet.
Black pins hold open the crepe, the worsted silk.
Baby wears a stiff, pleated paramatta
dress, embroidered with black thread.

The sidewalk blocks rise up like Judgment Day
(as conceived of) in the Renaissance.
Lidded marble boxes tossed, sepulchers
busted open like the tree bed's cobblestones.
All those little Resurrections!
Seeds, maggots, fat, wet screaming slugs
now dried, wrapped, tucked-in and trussed
forever in Eternity's satin stuffs.

MAKING JELLY, WESTPORT, CONNECTICUT

The Concord leaves shrivel pale and curled—yet
their engines burgeon and bubble: hot potentialities
of liquidsugar empurpled Love.
When the gift was new, their globes burst green.
Now boiled into a vibrant mash, it swings white,
white then *magenta* in a cheesecloth sling—the stain
that blasted through was like a sunset or a map.
Or dappled blood rushing to a bruise.
And the stench!
A pungent, otherworldly vegetal stringency.
Our window overlooked the mystical pear tree
where one could wind one's mind back to Eros's spring.
At midnight, the mad dog pulled up the roots
of fifteen sandy peonies.
Beyond the terraced pond of clays and silts, a hundred
hot autumn skies somersaulted backwards and away,
claryifying the red light of our Indian Summer days.
Robin eggs in a dog-hair nest. Fragile beads of baby blue
found whole by the well or sometimes broke in two:
dried albumen in two ragged cups, a yellow yolk crust
hardened to an ochre-orange streaked with greeny-blacks.
The wooded triangle birthed white carpet fluff
and bluebells in the shape of hooks.
Our crab apples? Cooked down many months before.
We jarred each, black-ended worm intact, until the mash
took on the color of unwashed baby flesh.

We added white sugar to this acrid soup, as now
the darkling liquid is nearly black. Will it set?
Will it hold? A blood pudding of the sugary kind.
A crude gruel, a viscous juice. A jarful of thickened
spoil plugged with a cap of paraffin.
Where is the dandelion salad to accompany our meat?
And the fiddleheads for this macerated sauce?
And the liver gastrique that hasn't a proper name?
Wine! Bring wine to the garden—and a butter knife!
We will eat our bread with this scant jelly, thinly spread
like a summer rain.

THE KINGDOM MIRROR

The secondhand mirror lay on the flatbed, uncovered,
roped in rags, blankets, newspapers, its poisoned face
a '70s Bowie glittery galactic field of fast weirdness.
Open, shiny-side up: it was a swivel on the puddle,
an underside to the afterlife we cannot know *now*.
The mirror: an open pupil on the Bay of Naples at noon.
Or it is a mirror in a market wheeled upright to shatter.
Glass is see-through until painted, then the harrowing.
The shine gulped down chaotic petals, pale spacecraft.
The poison was like crushed tinfoil in a cat's eye, gilded
on the back surface that you may never ever while *alive*.
The mirror is a doorway or a portal or a pool.
A layer of poison buoys the glitter and the aluminum.
Chaotic Bowie baby, that paint is a black sore's
reflection on the underside of everything; it reflects
one's self in shards, as in *skaters* where once a *white pond*.
We stood the mirror up and walked it like a man,
corner by corner down the drive, it walked, side to side,
scrambling trees, twisting houses, warping away the world
on its way to hang on the hallway nail of my mind.

REVERSE COMMUTE THROUGH GRAND CENTRAL: ALL DOORS OPEN AT WESTPORT

Days begin at the stone ship, its bow-spit eagles
in shaggy feather pantaloons remain nameless
unlike the Library's lions, Patience and Fortitude.
At the triumphal helm, a central spasm of rock,
one raptor sits crowned with a ten-inch snow hat.
Wrapped in a concrete American flag. He is a patriot.
(In its claws, a half-dead common house cat.)
Iron rats ran up bolted wires as the living ones
moved loathsomely down the tracks, drinking slops
from puddle-troughs, squeaking like baby violins.
Pigeons brayed like donkeys and some flit across
the green cosmological roof, with its one black brick.

The stars of Grand Central are falsely fixed.

Aquarius pours starry effluvium for Pegasus to drink.
The backward trains leave at six, so down the ramps
to the brindled bread and hot cups to be shot out
on the NW tracks toward Hell's Gate and Connecticut,
Native for "place by the tidal river," a river that ebbs
and flows as the Atlantic Ocean sucks and rolls.
Once a beach town, now moneymen congregate,
to talk of Truth and Principles of Human Management.

These are the games of snow and ice!

Not interested in excellence or ownership of their kind,
only the excellent chaos of this unstructured snow—
the blustered chaos as it blows and falls, like Stevens's
mind of snow—this snow thinks illogically, it
thinks slantedly and resists all corporate languaging.
Now, the snow has a polished-cotton sheen—a crust
baked under boughs outside these monetary offices:
the mind resides inside one, and one is filthy rich.

THE DAIRY STILL STANDS: NYALA FARMS, WESTPORT, CONNECTICUT

The dairy still stands, now the Shangri-la
of a megalomaniacal moneyman, on land called Nyala,
named for an African antelope seen by a forefather's son.
Now, one shot by crossbow is mounted on our founder's wall.
A fat man at his fun. This is Connecticut's greenest sleeve.
Greens Farms, verdant as the Hanging Gardens of Babylon!
No: this is no pensile paradise, and money is not the Truth.
Here, a Revolutionary graveyard past the gutterbanks
(by the connector and Sherwood Island's salted culms).
All the reeds and cattails by Greens Farms Station bend
in opposition to the direction of the commuter cars.
The trains cast off violent, slanting winds, both ways.
The dairy's well once hid the congregation's chalice cup.
These New England beaches cut our childhood feet; still,
we rode the Compo cannons bareback toward the Sound.
We didn't stop for common things; no, we searched
for arrowheads and sucked on fallen feathers on the hill.
Whole robins' eggs we cupped and warmed. We blew
hot breath into our hands to make the protein hatch.

Now the corporate plaza level is best for aggressive games.
On this grassy course we could perform dressage and haute école …
Airs above the ground! Croupade and ballotade,
mezair or courbette.

Or a breakneck steeplechase, or a puissance jumping race.
Only champions, thunder haunched and fearless, need apply.
The park's windows reflect yellow reeds and so recede
like Bishop's buildings of wheat melting into the sun.
From here to the water is not far to climb.
You can see the inlet from the highest, greenest hump.
Come help me find that tributary, the stream where a ship
sailed and hid itself among the trees. The passage
is more narrow now, this stream that feeds the Sound.
See, when the trains blow through, freshwater snails
hang upside down off the hulls of the commuter cars.

SPRING SONG IN THE FALLEN CATHOLIC'S YARD, WESTPORT, CONNECTICUT

In the pond, amphibian eggs stuck to the slimed stick,
clumped in the crux of its divining fork,
clear clusters jerking with tadpole life,
black raspberries of metamorphosis cleaving,
cleaving into our gambling spring.

The slippery stick, we swung it like a thurible,
wafting incense at our feet and above our heads.
We waved the stick over hairy, snail-faced fiddleheads.
Waved it back and forth, angering a hive.
We crushed symmetrical ferns smelling of cucumbers.
We stripped leaves from stems with our fingertips,
then whipped the naked switches against the grass.

We whipped the world into fresh-cut green.

Beguiled by the token, spring snatches and blunts,
turning seeds evenly in their holes, baking
them in pockets of gaseous glee. The wait deforms,
elongates white stems of albino alkaloid straw.
Crimped cords slit up, bowed like horses's heads.

We swung and swung the peppered jellymass, that trident
of quivering green morass, that glistened like a brain.

Each spot a tremulous crucifer, a thought, jerking in a ring.

In winter, ice needles seed the mud and bind dead leaves.
Now, last year's peepers play one thousand violins.
Their throats balloon, freshwater globes a pin could pop
(to deflate their song, and leave a ragged bag behind).
To hurry up the song, we shook the egg mass in a jar.
We shook the eggs in pondwater until the egg sacs burst.
Then we watched the flidgets hatch, swim briefly,
then go belly-up and float.

Suddenly the fragrance of wood violets! Is this the scent of hope?

THE LONG HOUSE, WESTPORT, CONNECTICUT

Behind the main house, through the tall hedge,
a dark path (well-worn through evergreens,
a fragrant interstice) was dark and cold
even in summertime. Freezing air lingered.
Shade made this a perpetually quiet place.
When the sticks spoke, we were afraid.

The pond froze, so we scratched infinity onto it with our blades.

Under the ice, wire armatures, jagged scrap, hoary hibernating frogs.

Half-submerged boughs tripped us on our skates.
Running on chipping toes, we spilt blood onto the ice.

We froze, West Wind. Broken teeth like ragged pinking shears.

Breathing in sharp air, giant icicles accrued and water
streamed from their massive trunks, then dripped
in drops that hung and froze to points. One wished
to find a blue jay trapped inside one—or a girl.

In spring, we examined wet spots under stones, noting
how silverweed turned to gold when plunged into water holes.

In summertime, wooly worms rained down from the canopies.

With first frost, we circled the pear tree thrice, tiptoeing
over cat and rabbit bones, and bones of birds and mice.

The rotting wood was chicken-wood to us, and the rhododendrons
blossomed into corn-kernel nosegays and single-stemmed boutonnieres.

Boughs cracked above our heads, snapping rhomboid kites of ice.

When will the Eastern Sun triumph over the Western Wind?

It was ever Easter in our yard. The ineffable in every
joint and hinge. The iron gate made noises in the wind.
I was ever thinking backward toward the other way.
Where wallpaper molts and evening ships come in.
Where the ivy climbed—as did the rose—nearly audibly.

THE WORMS OF WESTPORT, CONNECTICUT

Thunder rolled with the yellowthroats, panicking
the windycocks pecking at the woody fringe.
Gold Caroligian minuscule issued from a European angel
standing inside twigs brocaded by spider webs.
Dressed in expensive clothes, the dead pine's limbs
were its skirts which swayed as the Being (being
so attenuated and tall) called the earthworms up
with a clap and the worms came, in crumb-catcher
lace collars, streaming sticky webs of crepe paper.
Trains, whales, wagon wheels bombed overhead,
scattering those yellownecks and the feverbacks.
Like a carillon of bells, the scene came in pieces and parts,
over days and decades; in the driveway puddle,
white worms spun like ones in vinegars and wines.
Rainwater-soaked, water-fed, when cut in two
both halves lived to crawl away from its opposite
like a human mind crawls away from its end.
One writes toward the worm, the white welter,
the purity of the hole—and its mineral meaning.
We'd poke them with a stick, then sever them right there.
Whole or broken they made lace-like imprints in the pulp.
With our thumbs we powdered the crispy holes.
Once, in lamplight, we saw them twist in chicken wood.
They ate deeply there and we were glad. But now,
worms fly when the birds go skyward, as we were told.
Or they glow, or they turn, or they climb a spectral stair.

The poem accretes, a regenerative worm. Remember
how we dreamt them whole after pulling off their horns?
We twisted some long, to dry to tines. And wove others
into a wormweave the angel wore in splendor as it stood
in the driveway calling in those pieces of the sublime.

SACRED GROVE: THE BARON'S LAND, WESTPORT, CONNECTICUT

Wood thrush in the Sacred Grove above the carpet
floor, it was scaly and damp with buggy drones,
mossed and slimed with crusted-over adherences. Leaf polyps.
Leaf dirt. Webby ground bowers. Mosquitoes and biting fleas
drank my alien rain—the salty nectar that is my life.

One could live a thousand years ago, or two. Or ten.

Bones exude a healthy sheen as they accrue, a buttery grease
glosses over the candy loam, the long marrow channels
can be cooked down with spring onions and fierce red
sugars extracted from the pigments of the flower's face.

When pressed, they make a wholesome oil, more delicious than the sun.

Here, the vaulting Sun blots out the Moon from noon to one.

(Bones grew long and greasy in the swollen nests—one witnessed
a nourishment of thickening plates, washed clean by stringent juice.)

Sun grows the bones, as I grew, long and lean and lone.

Now hemlock gags the crows and turns the river green.
The thrush, spastic in its seat, blurts out its nervous, unfed needs.

Was it not a wren?

Was it not a worm?

Look, the honeysuckle bush! The cross-eyed tiger lilies' antennae buzz!

On the iron bench, a hairy caterpillar rolls inside the rain.

(What *is* that in the slimy garden pool?
A supple newt and a browning butterfly net.)

Now there is a pond within a pond,
one richly layered in sleeping frogs.

Stationed on the Baron's Land, to good-bye to what I knew,
I saw sticks—skeletons of tiny men, choked with twiny gags.

I had followed the row of pear trees to the Baron's land,
to find brown toads fried to leather in the summer grass.
Bitten at the ankles by a whine of biting bugs, I declared:
"All the fleas as they are in God are higher than all the angels
in themselves."

As it was read here first, by the waterfall and the municipal pipe.

THE BIRDS FLEW

They flew away, always away,
ticking their heads, constantly,
over the salt lot and the coal pipes,
to the distraction of our brains.

Beyond gravel pits, over the rusted chutes
and deep pools of dormant radicals.
Into the nether channels by the graving docks.

It was the points reached beyond the rooftops
that made their flight so hurtful,
that made their flight itself seem like a cage.

Birds pulse like globs of molten metal streaking off a sun.

He calls them back, his bag of birds,
his disarticulated flying scrim.
He is anchor to these sailing ships,
drifting on waves of wind.

They make a pattern in the evening air,
flying habituated, concentric rings
around the single source: his hand.

At the evening hour he climbs
to move his pieces in unison, to carve
a shapely gesture in the void.

They don't break for freedom
toward the chemical stream to ride the winds
fueled by migrating monarchs.

No. In their final arc, they fly
straight back to their cage.

I WALK FROM STEEPLE TO STEEPLE

You diagram promises by your advancements
but leave bad things behind—germy wings.

(World like a large drum beaten by soft things.)

I've spun unlike the lilies without proper goals,
toiled in wrong ways, it was the wrong difficulty
I sought.

                    Stunning the newborn things, all
these babies baking in their brains or playing
in the fronds in their throes.

The steeples were needle-like in their insistence
that the answer was always up, yet with gusto
one walks the paved streets under the boiling sun.

(We live in the world with the bird and the whale.)

Despite the hemlock on the hill. Despite the crow.

I watched the movement of the birds exact diligence
            of no consequence but description,
heavenly description, of things fluted and feathered,
things flying liquid and high.

They cleave and cluster, break then roll, corrosive mites
infest their underwings, staining skin hidden from my eye.

Behind my back, the hooded rill of woods.

(Sun gavels the clouds; rain pounds the underdrum.)

Birds are the lilies. The will is the sickle. Birdsong
over the Willsong, one whistles loudly on the bluestone,
especially through long rains, though also in the sun.

One wears it as a crown—the sun and its wreathing song.

(We are in a big drum, pale spring, beaten by soft underwings.)

Above, birds flying in circles and common-seeming serpentines.

ALL THE SHIPS HAVE COME AND GONE

By the tidal inlet, slime stains the waterwalls
an aberrant, abnormal green,
a mossy smear of chemical phosphorous
(disseminated by widemouthed industrial drains)
in which tiny plants take residence
—clover leafs with minuscule hairy roots—
sending clear sucking tubes into the jellymass.

Soaps impregnate the stinking banks.
(In my mind's waterways, there is the "Indian in his glade …")
Poisoned sluice plump with bacterial froth and synthetic burrs,
the fragrant waters of the soapy rivulet flow
past the clock tower, over the Lapane's riversnake, around
the pylons, their immense bolts screwed so tight
one will need a blasting-fire tool—that will drop sparks
                                        at your feet—to enter.

Painted-over padlock: You cannot insert a key.
A cutter comes to release the locked machinery.
Less grand than the girdered bridge with its cathedral's choir!
Come to our poisoned place and join our humble Assembly.

Below the bulbous bollards and enormous
balls of waxed rope, the particles abate,
metal settles in the creek and rusts the clam beds red.
These are the meats you must not eat.

O but a swan swims singly, paddling its paddle feet
(a swan that I now call Emily's swan).
It nibbles at the mossy walls, its underbelly stained chartreuse.
Nibbles like minnows at the greasy layer of human waste.

Are there visions of masted ships in these crooked trees?
And what they carried here and what was made?

Do you run softly and flow, or do you only bubble and stagnate?

So many ships have come and gone.
So many varied ships with varied freights.
Sailing past the retracting bridge and its octagonal house
with rounded windows, a turreted tower, so unlike
and yet so similar to the one occupied by Yeats.

THE NINTH STREET BRIDGE OVER THE GOWANUS CANAL, BROOKLYN, NEW YORK

This thimble is out of round. Moldy lamb bones
and sour chocolate cakes! What does it take to make
a sugar turn? The butter is the frothy loam
that births the spores and nourishes their tubes.
It is a rusted metal meal we eat. Pearloid plastic
perfumes condensed to viscous cruddy froths
float down the crud canal, with its crud banks,
woven wooden sides and humped embankments
of shaggy historical and shipwrecked waste.
These rusted screws will not unscrew.
They smelt and soldered the finials; little church
steeples were poured and baked and broken off.
Here you can dig up dagger heads and iron balls
& bucolic Brooklyn grape clusters in trident shapes.
These lab emeralds are more beautiful than our sun.
And these gears are minor planets with clicking blades,
caterwauling across the sky, weeping, whining noise.
The syncopated bell by the bascule bridge sings *ding,*
ding, ding as a ship doth pass and everything must stop.
The ship's progress was truly like a funeral dirge.
Metal nets were cast and hung like iron flags.
Nets of tonnage, link, and weave, slam and slam
and slammed the crazy, wretched subway overpass.
Jam a wrench into the clicking machine by the purple lake,
hot with tanning gas and contemporary garbage juice.

Chalk whites mingle with industrial grades of gray.
This snaking, befouled river stinks and kinks,
staining its cement apron a sickening chartreuse.
At my feet, a metal earth has a metal moon.
Lift your head high: these rooftops are made for dancing,
under a Lalique moon in tightly-bodiced silk shirts,
as the mixer below turns like a foggy centrifuge.

IN THE DEEP DANK DARK, THE MAGNOLIA

Where are the songs of Spring? Ay, where are they?
—John Keats

Misread the directive in its veins,
and took for cues the manmade heat of a subterranean
room to declare the season's here—

(Metallic odors issued from motor parts and dead machines.)

Though the woods were bare and the ground was stiff,
roots torn through the burlapped sac tied in strings.
Tripped too soon, the calendrical buds opened their seals,
tricked by the oily warmth of the underspace,
compacted fragrant whorls of white shot forth, emitting
perfumed molecules of green and chartreuse juice.
When we descended the damp stairs, the thing was ghastly
in its premature opening, its thrusting
very wrong and wild and thin: white petals shot out
from knots of gnarled green, like bladed faces
whose wisps were wants when their thirst began.

Stale snow hardened around the house.

The blossoms' sweet smell mimicked something dead,
though the flowers had a hopeful shine and nearly cast a light.

Many sweating clusters opened and closed, opened closed,
stuck in Spring so far from Spring.
Forever distorted, their see-through, stinking wings,
mimic so many stunted potentialities enslaved
as are each of us, dying for our hoped-for Spring.

Declivities and small, wet seepages fooled a green thing to its grave.

THE GLASS FLOWERS AT HARVARD

Not being a superior person, I paid to visit Harvard's flowers,
the ones of sand and pigment—encased in exhibition
vitrines of a sister substance, but this one transparent
and so plain, that viewing them challenged one directive
for how to see—darkly, darkly as we go (yet in the name of clarity).

Under sheets of industrial glass: a catalog of botany.

Here a Mormon Heaven or a vision of the thing.
Each floral atom reconstituted wholly in that Realm.
Nothing left out, no leaking cell, no ruptured vein.

Here specimens presented whole again, but only in a broken way.

No damage gone; none healed. Necrotic kill glassily cascades,
and chewing lice bubble up resembling sugar crumbs at the crux
of a forked and hairy stem.

Forever the forsythia's blistered stalks' polyps full of sticky rain.

Here are biting bugs that leave a stain, bugs that tunnel,
insects that bore, insects with horns and hollow, pipetting tongues.
The Venus secretes viscous digestive mucilage from its sideways jaws
where sits a glass housefly forever about to be eaten.

Stuck in the succulent's arid pores, the needles of the cactus
will surely break if touched, and absolutely they will draw blood.

My breath across the glass made a dewy intersection at the seam.

In time, we moved on to another room, and farther up the Great Chain,
to view sea creatures of a thousand names, to see inside a mollusk's heart,
and a sea worm's androgyny, to ring the bell of a glassine jelly's dome
with its poisoned tendrils hanging down from what we call its brain.

BLAKE'S HORSES OF INSTRUCTION (FOR MY RENTAL HORSE IN PENNSYLVANIA)

Picking our way across the icy hill in serpentines,
                                                  the string of hired horses
ripped past thick thorns cemented hard (with the sap of life).
Never far from highway or from office park, they trod,
their stoic heads, indifferent and the same.

They know these trails. And the direction home.

One ear forward and one ear back signals: attention!
But I cannot control him with my legs or with my seat.
He follows the horse ahead like Good King Wenceslas
followed his servant on the Feast of Stephen.

Through an orchard of apples with sterile skyward sticks,
we climbed into a scraggy forest scarred with trails.

Can we break from the trodden path? Jig, jig: this is all you know.

These horses loll their eyes, ignore switch and spur,
execute an unengaged and weight-skirting shallow trot.
Such dusty, unbrushed manes and clotted winter fur!

The slightest turn east, and suddenly we are headed back,
each horse swiftly *cantering* into the gait called *galloping.*

I tied the reins to let him race the pack and win.

Now he stands proudly squared and gravely loitering.

Barn kittens rubbed their skulls against the dirt
and leapt around his hooves.

Put the saddle on the beam. Snap the hairy saddle pad.
Breathe in the hay dust static in the beams.

Flakes for the weanlings locked behind the gate.
Flakes for the sound ones tearing up the ring.

My sweaty charge is old and blows with sodden back.
Even so, he is mythic to my mind. On the side bone,
an eye globe, a clear lens of oceanic sight contained.
Pooled hazels and blacks, the visions in his bonehead
must be thoughts. His withers move like pistons.
His tail is a thousand flagellants and waxed guitar strings.
Body barrel a blood-bearing furnace: a cold soldier's bed.
Hooves clogged with mud. His mane, a fragrant fringe.
His mane is his flag. Bend to the left, bend to the right.
He tongues the snaffle bit and churns a cruddy froth.

Look: He shifts, sweating, hard-whiskered, and he sways.

RETURN YOU TO MY SISTER, NATURE

That well is deep and purely drawn with a freezing sterling cup.

Steam rises from the stabled blood.

Metal harnesses crimp the beasts' slavering mouths.

Lord, it was so difficult to discern if those were swallows,
golden swallows, or larger, darker birds,
flying as they were in your red eye,
distorted so by the angle of the sun.

At first, certainly, they were golden!

Scissoring the air, snipping it to bits.
Turning, turning, rolling through the sky,
squandering the luster of their germy underwings.

Whole flocks once rose in unison from the ground.

Now, a billion charnel flakes—lifted off and flown.

Once high, the logs were dashed so cruelly
in our eyes, weird winds stippled the wounds
(so the blood was always fresh and hot).

Now it boils and thickens, boils and rots.
I hope they do not suffer, especially the small furred ones,
and also the big bony ones with hooves for hands.
Their cheekbones are so sharp and their intestines tend to twist.

The birds we now find feelingly have latches on their lids.
The birds of metal plates and slicing wings do not need our care.
We leave the high windows open for them, now, wide open to the air.

WHAT HAPPENS IN THE THIRD GARDEN?

You cry at the Sun Door then rush into the light.

Is it feathered there—is it lined with pliant mousy fats?
Is this where smell and sight combine? Are the roses lions' heads?
Are the roses ornamental, or is their architecture more instructional?

They grow in rows from here and cast tall shadows on the fence.

Does the sun smell radiant underneath?
Does the earth smell like garlic greens and ramps?
Or small wild oniony plants with slimy skins?
Or peppery smoking pollen puffer sacs?

Are you fully realized under the forsythia?

(By the church gate with the pointed spikes, you wearing your warning bell.)

Were you steeped in gore—fang sunk in the gristle and squeak of wing?

You hear the sound of water boats and horns in the river to the east,
smell salts, eat at the white newness of the grassy roots.
Your milky nictitating membrane alien as a goat's eye.

You run toward me from the garden as I start to clap.
(Up the slanted staircase as I call you back.)

Clap, clap, clap. Clap, clap, clap. Clap, clap, clap.

My gift, a bird, held gingerly so not to completely kill.

One large wing fans from your open mouth—its yellow feet are curled.

I beat the bird from your needle teeth,
then kiss you on the lips exactly where the bird had been.

THE WASPS' HOUSE: THE HOUSE IN WESTPORT, CONNECTICUT

Mortared by macerated wood-pulp effluvium,
a paper palace hangs.

The young queen spun her eggs and hatched her grunts.

The wasps drag paralytic legs through the air,
those long wisps most weeping, strange, and ill.

They build a giant house, a birch-like comb of paste,
lifted high to dangle by the rotation of their wings.

The workers build. The house is heavy, though papery.

It is a lantern with no light. A white balloon,
a papier-mâché head with a dirty mouth hole
jammed under the eaves of the foursquare.

A clown face with collapsed, lopsided lips sucking in living balls of light.

Wasps hover, drop, rise, hang, crawl continually into the hole.

They build by instinct this paper pleasure dome.
They build with white and gray pastes, then they stain the opening,
now an easy entrance for a nozzle of poison smoke.

Look now: Toothless, stinking piehole: your busy head is black.

I COULD NOT SEE WHAT FLOWERS WERE AT MY FEET

The world is fallen and my friends are false.

This amber oak leaf has a hard gall, a spot.
In weight it was a spider's egg spidering eggs
as if from a cotton ball, I imagined
spider babies sailing together on protein threads.

But it was a stone, in fact, a hard knot, dried.
Dead. I let go that leaf. It spins now in the sick waters
of the drink, under the bascule bridge:
canker, sick spot, false friend.

Spiders fall to fry on the aluminum slats,
like Lowell's and Edward's did, boiling on hot bricks.
Spiders now toasted to legless, crispy discs.

Up here, in the wet gutters,
tiny deformed trees grow from the steeping slop.
Up high on the scaffold hung with metal nets,
church bells ring a minor scale out-of-tune.

The priest poisons cats the corner neighbor feeds,
though he speaks of Augustinian love in circular
symbols and horns, the tinkling tassels of human balm.

In a recess, a chalk Virgin, placed by atheists,
cups leprous hands in prayer. In sun
my lenticular Jesus moves his face
up, then down, up, then down.
Yet when examined, the picture was not truly lenticular.
His eyes neither opened nor closed;
His crown was a horn-like growth.

False Mary, false God, false Christ. False friend.

I admire the black flowers of the iron gates,
and collect a flaking bouquet for your internal grave.

And my single deformed leaf? I see it spinning in its place.
Good-bye. Now sink completely and disintegrate.

HORSEMANSHIP: TIE SIDING, WYOMING

Held him by the mouth, lifted his head high.
We swayed. There was suction at his hooves.
With a cluck to canter, we sank, gained footing, and rocked,
climbed to harder pastures, threw back clods of earth.

His haunches moved with oiled locomotion.
Leathers swayed with his gait as it gathered.

Through briars, rough scales, dead leaves we bolted.

Dropped weight to his center, urged him forward,
keeping contact, regardless—I let him have his head.

He let loose drumrolls beneath me. I stunned in his falters.

We rode in a fever, then called for collection.

We galloped a circle, a slash slanted inward.

With soft eyes, I rode him. (Not hard, for the target will break you.)

Then we walked, threading our way through a stand of white birches.

(Milkweed and thistles snagged in his forelock.)

We rode past the homestead bordered by aspens.
Then past a dead cow struck dead by lightning.

We cooled our bloods down in a cricket-bright pasture.

Four lives in a meadow: two equine, two human.
The meadow, a memory. The day moon in error.

THE FIG TREE WASP

Beyond the scaffold's leveled plank
and the double ladders, beyond the pipes
and shutters, pails, hammers, screws, tarps,
plastic sheets now hang hammocks loaded
                                        with dirty rain.

The backyard, a junkyard.
The dying fig tree lives the life-span of a man.

The trees bristled as the birds sang.
Our sky shone like aluminum,
like galvanized buckets full of rain.

Sun shone on the beaten creases and rivets.

One squinted up at the metallic brilliance.

A wasp enters a fig.

It lies down with the white seeds of the sac, the flesh
the color of tobacco juice and amber candle wax.
This wasp is male. He has no wings.
He performs machinations for the queen, crawls
through the fig's stern digging toward death,
like a morning glory trumpeting its inanity.

Overnight in the dirt pail: toadstools.
They hover like ghouls, fleshy pipes sprung up.

By evening, they are gone.

Too easy a metaphor for life, since,
in truth, most creatures are stubborn in the sun.
Like a seahorse loaded down with eggs.
Like worms in a bucket of poisoned dirt.

The morning glory is money to the man who sees one.

WATER AS WORLDSHIP:
IL NAUFRAGAR M'È DOLCE IN QUESTO MARE

It is too large to climb into, the grappling and the squall.

Unclear where the edges lie, the doors, the ends and tips,
the burnt, greasy rope butts. And the tools: hooks and claws.
And the canvas sails sewn with hard industrial thread.
Giant creatures move underneath us,
bigger than our brains—with hearts of seawater, their ape-
eyes watch our maritime activity, winking baggy lids.

Terrible how the rain falls sideways, entering all our eyes.

All the trusses are buffeted and blown, the righting wheel's
spun hard left, though the ship is disassembling—blown
far past the white weeds into woods waterlogged by rain.

(Too large and baggy, this watery trope.)

Worldwater? Cosmic tree? The worldship? The cosmos in its entirety?

Rivers run under streets in Rome. At San Clemente, water bubbles
up from prison blocks and pavement stones. Metallic sediments
and noxious gases feed a subterranean world of gates and doors.

The waters of the Tree of Life run in threes and fours, then form
the oceans of the globe.

Do these oceans then water the worldtree sheltering the world?

These plinking ancient waters flow under city streets; above,
pigeons fly habituated loops over short-bricked domiciles.

Waterfalls and rivers, channels and creeks: water is the world.

Where are our groves and piney white-sand woods? Look!
Tiny birds dance on the deck's minarets by the spinning wheel.

With bright leaves in their beaks! Land! It's near, but where?

THE DEER PIT IN AN IOWA COUNTY, TWENTY-FIVE YEARS AGO

Dead deer in the dump pit in Iowa.
There, a bullet flew past my ear
as twenty-six carcasses rotted haphazardly,
in lyric time, upside down and sideways,
running across the deep dirt bowl,
in a band of action and of laws.

One walked in hunting grounds beyond,
into a field without signs but truck tracks.
At the edge, I sank into the grass
where a hunter's bullet flew past my ear.
It whined, like an insect sucking air.

No smell from the pit, the heat a desiccant,
their failures dried, wacked rubbernecks.
One was so new then, and so afraid.
Birds tormented, wired to eyeball and brain.

My stomach was a blood bowl, removed.

Once a deer's stomach on the Merritt Parkway
in Connecticut. Or did I see that in the pit?
Moiled mud, red fur. Overturned blood bowl.

Sharp hooves split, deer hit or shot. Heads
backward, legs crumpled and strewn. Babies,
several, their white fur moving in the sun.

I see old attempts at this, the dead deer running
crazily uphill, downhill, flies, dead flies, years,
such waste, that dirt bowl with its fauna frieze.

I typed with a faded ribbon then; now, fifty-two dead deer.
Already at the milkweed and the scrabble heads,
those clenched ribbed undercups of the Queen.
At the edge of a county, inside a municipal square.

Already the bullet flying out of its plastic shirt.
Already a hunter mistaking a person for a deer.

SAILING NORTH TO THE BEGINNING: A DEAD MOOSE, GREEN LEDGES, LITTLE DEER ISLE, MAINE

I return to the windy pits and the white rivers,
the freezing waters up North, where a limpet waits
and a gull, where the land is not land, more web
or sponge—some chit born there, some red seed
dropped, a human tooth grown into a tree.
There are many winds, not one cut into lengths
like a ribbon or string—winds from the North
push treetops and sailboats, until winds die
in the schooners's sheets on Eggemoggin Reach.
When the schooner stops, halyards clink the spar.
A black boat in stasis, before the suspension bridge.
Black sails in irons—an image of obsessive thoughts.
Look overboard and you will see granite blocks
that slid off the quarry's flatboat on their way South.
Rough rectangular blocks made smooth in that water
as if my mind was made of underwater streams, or
each thought a Reach, though water has weight,
unlike my thoughts that torment, then evaporate.
Thoughts are black flies, and also green flies that bite.
Filthy clones, spastic maniacs with panoptic lens heads!
They land on a ship's curve to see the entire world.
One fly, one thought, of the moose our fathers found,
a carcass from the Reach that nothing could revive.
They carried it to the woods to spare us children
the bull's upturned antlers half gone from its skull.

When first lifted, an insane stream of flies poured out,
my father said, and more emerged when the corpse
was thrown. Flies exploded from the final jolt,
and formed a shape, like an enormous sun-blotting sail,
that hung in the air for a moment, before
quickly resettling, as if being reabsorbed.

SPRING STARTS EARLY IN THIS FROZEN SPHERE: A POEM ON MY FIFTIETH BIRTHDAY AFTER A DRAWING OF A TOMB

All night milk leaked from wind-blown seeds
wrapped in mineraly mica robes, cold birthday,
having frozen, thawed, and froze for fifty years.
February comes on rough with Imbolc time,
warmish in the hump, aerated by spring winds.
Here in this house of roots and dirt—we'd pruned
and broke through smoky February snow, the month
a friend says sounds like a flower, very cold.
(One conical and pale and fluted but not frilled.)
Or like Bishop's Florida, the state with the prettiest name.
Another sang February wears make-up, pale green,
like Eliot's cosmetic powder dusting his evening-face.
(He played the corpse, dug up, sitting at a dinner plate.)
February prepares the inside of the house to contend
with what's without, as Stevens wrote: Wars. Evenings.
Hoarfrost. Dogs. A pale flower with a paler throat.
Another sings February is lovely, lovely fragile February
like skinwings, or a chink of lightweight charcoal
spinning on an earthfast rock.
                                        Burnt bits, tinkling
chimes the wind rearranged and then carried off.
(I understand that harder things vanish with less force.)

In February, one rouses for the floods that came before,
as odd angles return of what light felt like, and how it
entered the forsythia and how voices were overheard.
Here, the woods drop kindling—logs, sticks, leaves—
dead dry things to smoke the snow tomb and keep warm
this seed, turning in its pocket for fifty years: an ember
in a frozen hole. A white flower with a paling throat.

IN THE WOODS BEHIND THE FLOODED YARD, WHERE ONE WAS ONCE NOURISHED AND INVISIBLY REPAIRED, WESTPORT, CONNECTICUT

We came to the wellhead in the needles
(some yellow from moisture, some brown from air)
and thirsted because there was no water, no cup.
Oxidized evergreen river pins carpeted the forest floor.
Above the well, a wooden structure still stood, as did
a small stone house positioned to protect the source.

Here four thousand suns rose and burned, at least.

In a vinyl teepee, we hung corn-silk boiled clean
and smoked dried out, dirt-red venison leaves.
We woke raw and ill, wanting fire and soothing fats.
Pitched by the compost pile, where the rabbits died,
those long-eared, spooky innocents infested with parasites,
I longed to have been taken from Connecticut
to Canada for rites of passage and feathered things.

Our neighbor's pond was once a garbage dump.

The dandelions looked ill, but they were here to fly.

We raked the paths and lined them with light stones.
Then we played the fallen tree for a springy fuselage.

And marched the plastic pumpkin head up and down,
a rattle filled with sugar balls—even the hollow stem.
Candy coats crunched like yellow yard-snail shells.
We watched inchworms follow the one in front
around an oval leaf, until all died and dried to points.
Their backs pricked up exactly at their pores.
Ants from the underworld built a granulated hump.
They moved our world to theirs in pieces and in parts.
Black ants carried down leaves, and Paul's cigar ash,
and Ruth's real hair, and Sean's steel guitar strings.

They have one child's fingernail of mine: no paint.

The front bushes made a cage, a whale-rib cage,
where children played Jonah, and others whipped
each other savagely until itchy welts sent us home,
turning bilious green and lapis lazuli,
and black and orange like a monarch's wing.

When pressed we said we'd fallen or had slipped.
Our battles were not from hatred, but from fear.

Behind the cage, orange-red sticks and spiraling
vine-y shoots made a thicket no sickle could thin.
Our rabbits' ears, pasted shut by sebaceous crusts,
grew too thin, then split to ribbons in the wind.

Twist off the root of the polyp's stalk. Vegetal abscess.
Swab the frothing spittle at the crux of those corky stems.
A profound perfume emanates from their tips.

In fall, sweating pumpkins collapsed into themselves.
In summer, crickets chirped a world of muted bells.

Bright green mosquito eggs, such tiny lily pads,
form a cruddy cradle-cap to the earth's mud broth.
We sat at the glacial rock we used for a tabletop.
Mica glittered like the sun the day the rock was made.
Both clear and black – we flaked it into shining piles.
We said these are the Lord's fingernails and prayed.
We incorporated death into our play, though He
lived in motor parts and upside down shopping carts.
And in Europe, in the world's wars, and in sick dogs.

We smelled it in the leaves we broke open with our feet.

In that woods, mosquitos were pop-up books, ruinous
starvelings, that banshee-wailed in our minds' ear.
Playing there was a kind of Hell, waiting for things
to fall that never fell. I made a tube of lipstick from a stick
for my Nefertiti lips, and set rock pots of unguents
and wands in slots and holes in a tree's surface roots.
My vanity. I knew it then; I know it more fully now.

Time is what Eliot said it was, ALL TIME is at once.
A bird calls from the forsythia, and that bird's call
snags a humid spot to reverberate back, and back. Such
amplified sound is from a future that will not come.
Once, by the stone well, I saw a metaphor take place.
I saw a bright green snake's length come off intact.
Skin floated off its back and rolled across the lawn like cellophane.

Now a lotus eater in a city of forgetfulness—at night
especially when the cats watch the smoke above my head,
I feel how under the garbage pond fresh water flows.
Unlike winter's buttonholes, those black ponds in dull rock.
Our neighbor's tiger lilies open wide their freckled mouths,
and lean across a wooden bridge to spit into the stream.
Above, the blue jay monitors all from the cockpit of the Japanese.

THE WATER PLACE: WORMS AND MENTOR

Come stingers, drift down from the paper dome,
and from the bell's lip, and from the sticky edge.

Mentor? Is this the rarity that rarity requires of one?
What a self-possessed soul possesses?

Down here the grass is white in the gray rain.

Bees come from combs and wasps from ashes.
Hornets fly from rocks and wet leaves, rise up
and out of stonewalls and rotten window sashes.
Wasps come from holes, fly up and out slowly,
they hover, distaining syrop for the grain and flake.

An apple is of great moral purpose, it falls
without grasping after fact, meaning it lives to rot;
one tunnels like worms through fallen apples,
two worms we are, hungry worms
worming our worm's way through to the core.

Over the stonewall, where the weak spring bubbles up
and sinks, there exists a doorway to the other place.

I still mope and linger where the earth crowns up.

Let's chase the coin down the water hole, chase the fox
down the hole, chase the dog, chase the water worms,
the thin worms that swim like eels with intent
toward the water trap. Such souls, these worms,
open feeding mouths that are their faces, opening
softly upon, and then devouring, the pulpy nest
of slimy withies at the bottom of this water place.

THE NEEDLES, GREEN LEDGES, LITTLE DEER ISLE, MAINE

Look how they tumble in the waves,
somersaulting close to shore,
not rotting on the floor.

Here my hand stirs the needles up,
one million chits and chips of rock.

Watching the sunny churn I thought:
these are from the upper woods,
green needles now the color of the dog's paw,
that rusty-amber hunting hound.

Needles fall from the Jesus-trees.
They exist to fall and stab this sunny pool.
The needles first turn signally,
then swirl together as a piece.

My hand, the sun, is in its place,
whipping up a centrifugal whirl,
making a watery, uninhabitable nest.

Go sink down, then assemble
yourselves together into a crown,
so that I can lift you out again.

A FEELING RARE AS A ST. KILDA WREN

It continued to rain in the trees after the rain.
As if the rain itself originated from the leaves.

A soft whistle. A door bowered in shade.

Rained above the domiciles in Elysium.
Now, true, the thickets and the scrub.
Many tender cups filled to their jagged brims,
their crisped lips too dry to drink, gray worms
like a parrots' parched and desiccated tongue.

Then came a feeling rare as a St. Kilda wren,
or as when the dry pomander fell and broke.
The Escher-like loveliness of its urchin insides,
like a Byzantine city inside a walnut shell!

Arboreal wonderments! Fat floats and fragrance falls!

A wind comes from the leaves. Is this the sun again?

THE NUREMBERG EVENT: GLOBES, CROSSES, AND TUBES

What?! Listen! The shapes emitted other shapes,
sending forth gleaming coils and cylindrical rolling
tubes that spat and hissed with urgent steam.

Rods, spheres, crucibles fought a battle in the air,
as the mothership came down with its baby dirigibles:
Balls and pipes. Crosses. Bars. Blood-colored X's
that spun in place, then turned into platters of soft gold.

Always at the center, the Sun, with its angry face.

Before this Sun, we had the Moon, hollow like a Bell.

One longed to ring it with a rock. One longed to pierce
its skin and release the water circling underneath the tin.

Crucibles crashed in the outerwoods, then vanished into steam.

What?! What spheres? What rods? Even in the rain?

What?! What?! And then you say a needle came? Yes.
A needle of heft and depth appeared and silenced them.

It came, do not doubt it. It came and ended things.

The shaft rose from sunrise and ran straight towards sundawn;
all saw it with big thickness and length. It is recorded. Be at rest.

God be with you. (*Hurrying home.*) Yes, yes, and also with you.

NOTES FOR THE NEEDLE

"The Sailor Cannot See the North, but He Knows the Needle Can" takes its title from a letter Emily Dickinson wrote to Thomas Wentworth Higginson. The poem references a sculpture titled *Two Slender Lines Excentric VI* by artist George Rickey that was once on the grounds of the Yaddo Corporation in Saratoga, New York. I had remembered the sculpture as being comprised of a single pole and a long wooden "needle" that spins by the force of a human hand, or a strong wind. In reality, there are two poles. It is now in a private collection.

"Back in the Province Lands" refers to the Province Lands, a protected stretch of land on the tip of Cape Cod.

"Coal Piles by the Canal: The Corbels of Coignet" references Francois Coignet's innovative lightweight concrete, patented in France during the 1850s. Coignet used concrete and molds instead of solid rock to create building facades, a much cheaper option. In 1872, the Coignet Stone Company built its eponymous building to showcase its product at 3rd Avenue and 3rd street in Brooklyn. Now this historical building is an office for a sprawling Whole Foods.

"By Order of the Eastern Star" is a Masonic fraternal order for women. My mother was a member as a girl. The poem uses some of the Order's ritual language.

The title "We Meet upon the Level and We Part upon the Square" is a saying in the Masonic order.

"Reverse Commute through Heaven: All Doors Open at Westport" and "The Dairy Still Stands: Nyala Farms, Westport, Connecticut" both reference a Randian hedge fund called Bridgewater Associates that has taken over my hometown.

In the poem, "Sacred Grove: The Baron's Land, Westport, Connecticut," the quote, "All the fleas as they are in God are higher than all the angels in themselves," is from Meister Eckhardt.

"All the Ships Have Come and Gone" references the control tower by the Gowanus canal. It is imagined as Yeats's Tower at Thoor Ballylee Castle. This poem is for Emily Wilson.

"The Glass Flowers at Harvard" refers to the glass botanical collection created in the late 1800s by Dresden glass makers, Leopold Blaschka and his son Rudolph. The first line references Marianne Moore's poem "Silence" where she writes: "My father used to say, / "Superior people never make long visits, / have to be shown Longfellow's grave, / or the glass flowers at Harvard." The reference to the Mormon Heaven is meant to suggest the totality behind the concept of a fully realized bodily resurrection, as in every atom will be reconstituted in the Celestial Kingdom.

"Sailing North to the Beginning: A Dead Moose, Green Ledges, Little Deer Isle, Maine" is for Kristin Schardt.

"A Feeling Rare as a St. Kilda Wren" refers to St. Kilda, a remote Hebridean island. St. Kilda acts as a mini Galapagos; its sheep carry Bronze Age DNA and the island has its very own wren.

In the poem "Water as Worldship" the subtitle is the last line from Giacomo Leopardi's poem "L'infinito." The line translates to: "It is sweet to drown in this ocean."

"In the Woods Behind the Flooded Yard, Where One was Once Nourished and Invisibly Repaired, Westport, Connecticut" is for Paige Griglun.

"The Nuremberg Event: Globes, Crosses, and Tubes" references a strange celestial event recorded in 1561 in Nuremberg, Germany. A broadsheet describes an aerial battle that took place on April 14th involving a variety of strange objects—globes, crosses, and tubes. Seen by hundreds of townspeople, the event was understood as a divine warning.

ACKNOWLEDGMENTS

Gratitude to the journals who published these poems originally:

Bennington Review
"We Washed Our Napkins
in the Soda Lake"

Boston Review
"To the Piano Burning on the Beach"

Denver Quarterly
"Back in the Province Lands"

Fence
"By Order of the Eastern Star,"
"We Went Hunting of an Evening"

Hampden-Sydney Poetry Review
"Sacred Grove: The Baron's Land,
Westport, Connecticut"

Hinchas de Poesia
"Rare as a St. Kilda Wren,"
"To the Saugatuck River and Its
Source at Sugar Hollow,
Westport, Connecticut"

Interim
"We Meet Upon the Level
and We Part Upon the Square:
Masons in the Family Recalled
by a Gowanus Brick Yard,"
"The Fabric: Bombazine,
Worsted and Warped,"
"Sailing North to the Beginning:
A Dead Moose, Green Ledges,
Little Deer Isle, Maine"

Ladowich Journal
"The Long House:
Westport, Connecticut"

The Literary Review
"Coal Piles by the Gowanus Canal:
The Corbels of Coignet,"
"I Walk from Steeple to Steeple,"
"Making Jelly, Westport,
Connecticut,"
"Spring Starts Early in this Frozen
Sphere: A Poem on My Fiftieth
Birthday after a Drawing of a Tomb,"
"What Happens in the Third Garden?"

On the Seawall
"All the Ships Have Come and Gone"

The Paris Review
"The Wasps' House: The House
in Westport, Connecticut"